A BOY WHO MADE MUSIC
The Extraordinary Life of
JOAQUIN RODRIGO

written by
Karen A. Wyle

illustrated by
Tomasz Mikutel

A Boy Who Made Music

The Extraordinary Life of Joaquin Rodrigo

by Karen A. Wyle
illustrated by Tomasz Mikutel

cover design by Tomasz Mikutel

ISBN 978-1-955696-36-4

Published in the United States of America 2024

Score for *Concierto de Aranjez* used by permission from
Ediciones Joaquin Rodrigo

This is the story
of a boy whose life
was changed . . .

and what he did about it.

Little Joaquin
was three years old,
and he had a
good life.

He had a mother
and father,
and
NINE
brothers
and sisters.

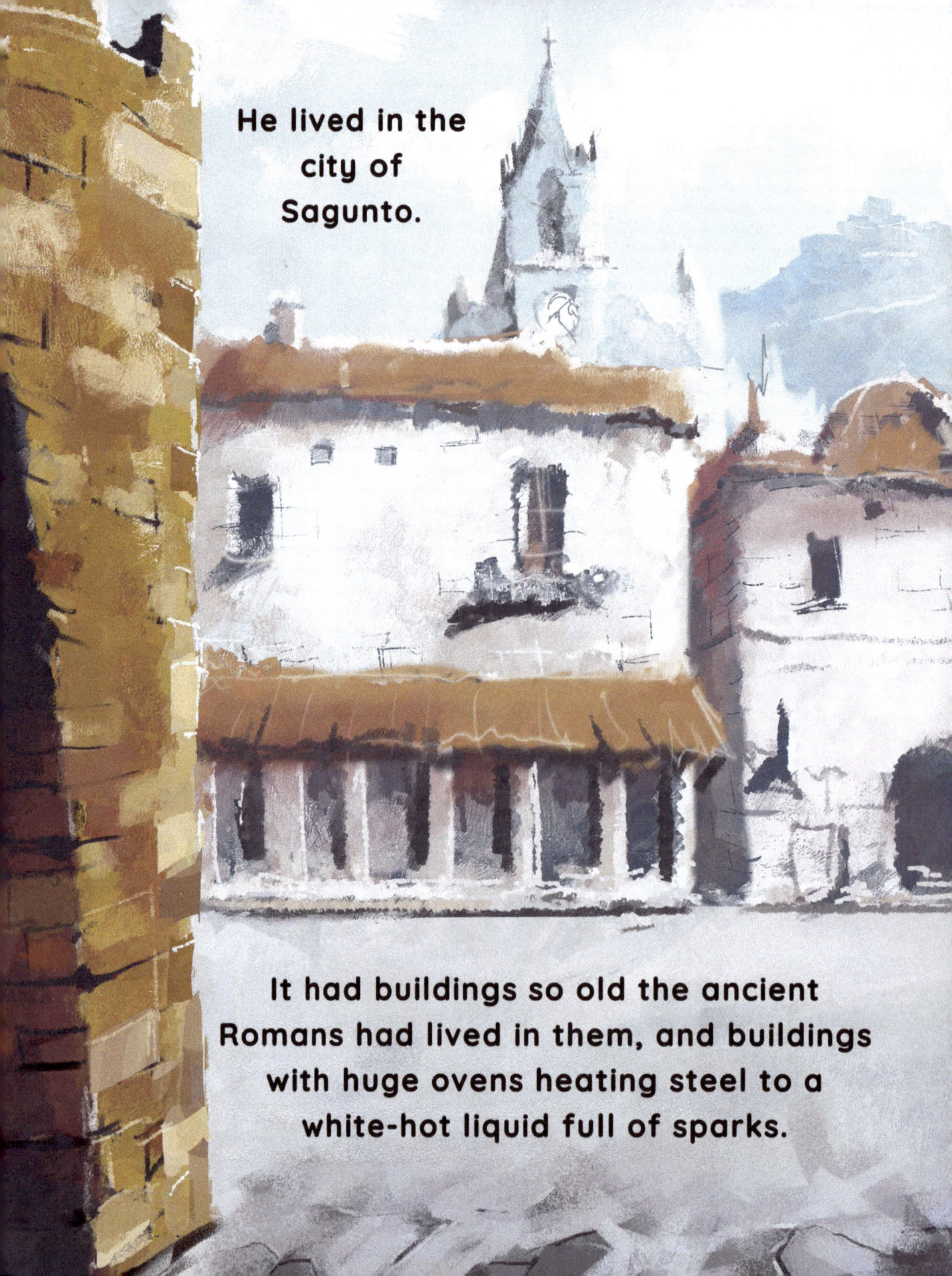

He lived in the city of Sagunto.

It had buildings so old the ancient Romans had lived in them, and buildings with huge ovens heating steel to a white-hot liquid full of sparks.

Then something happened to Joaquin,
something no one — not his mother,
not his father, not his brothers and sisters,
and not Joaquin — had ever expected.

When Joaquin was three years old, he
got very sick with an illness
called diphtheria.

Today, we have a vaccine to keep children from getting diphtheria, but in 1904, when Joaquin got sick, there was no such thing.

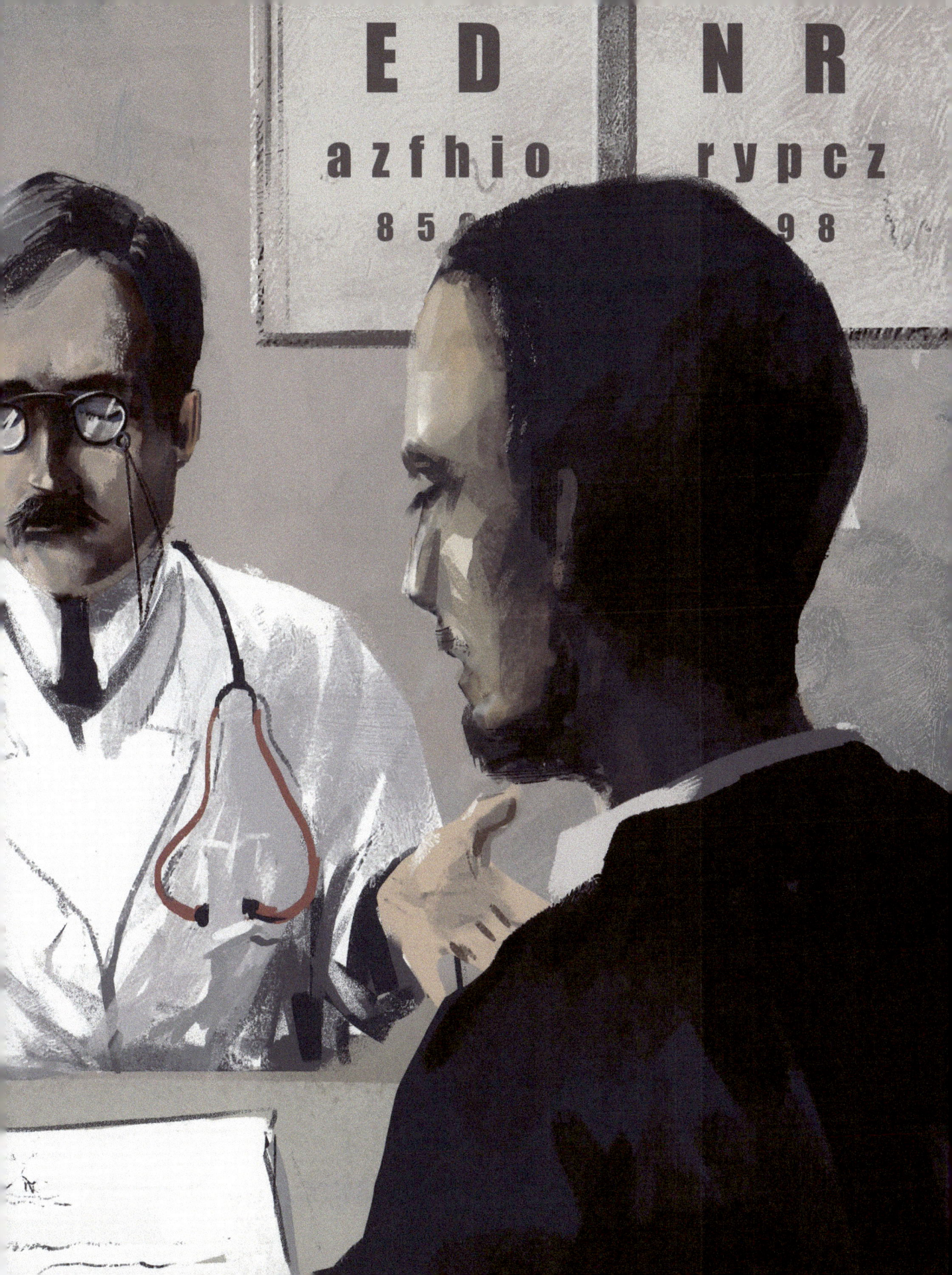

By the time Joaquin felt better, his
whole world had changed.
Because he was almost blind.
He couldn't see shapes,
not even the furniture in his home,
not even his bed.

He couldn't see faces,

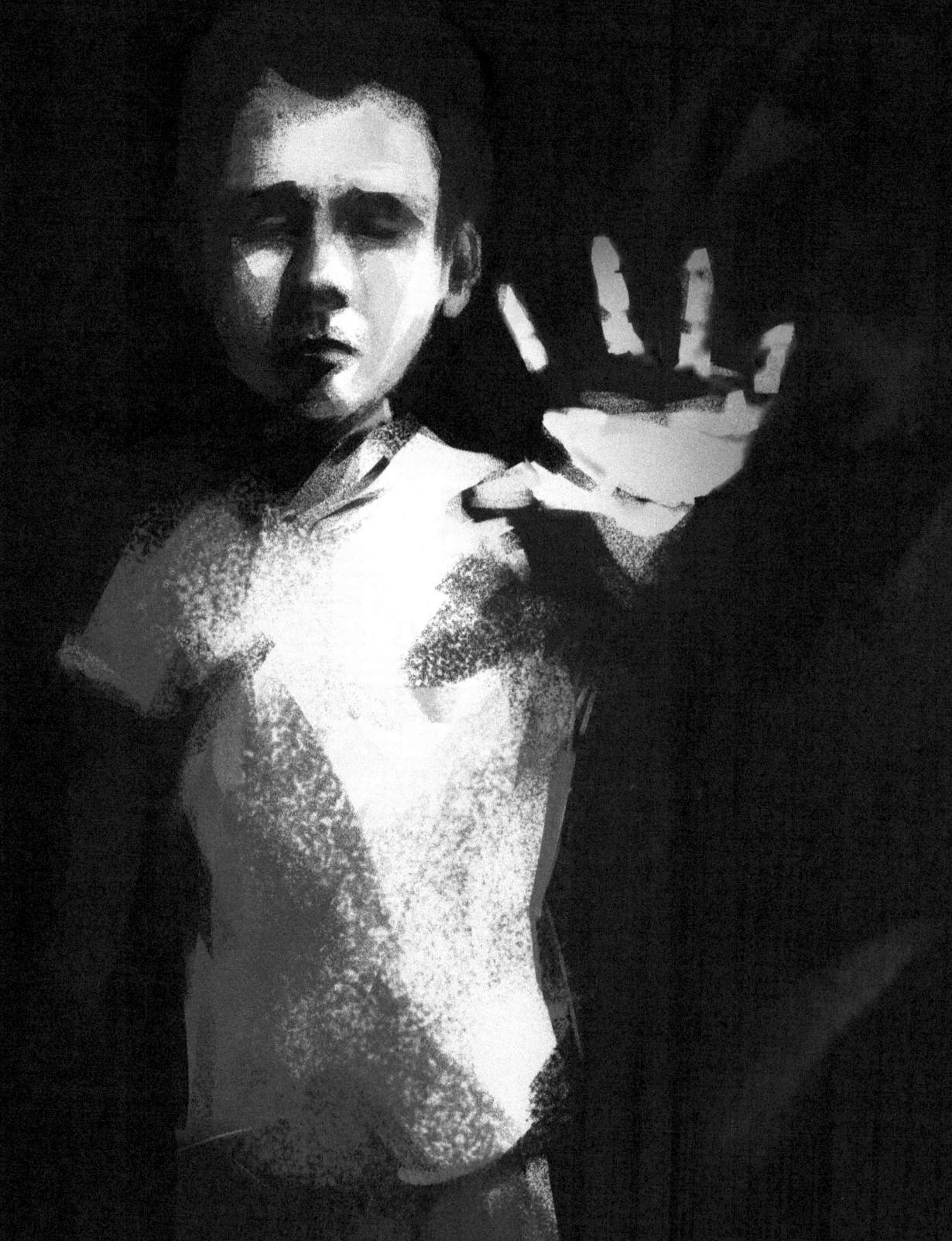

not even the faces of his mother and father
and brothers and sisters.

He couldn't see colors,
not even blue and green and red.

All he could see was
darkness and light.

But Joaquin could still hear.
And he remembered what he heard.

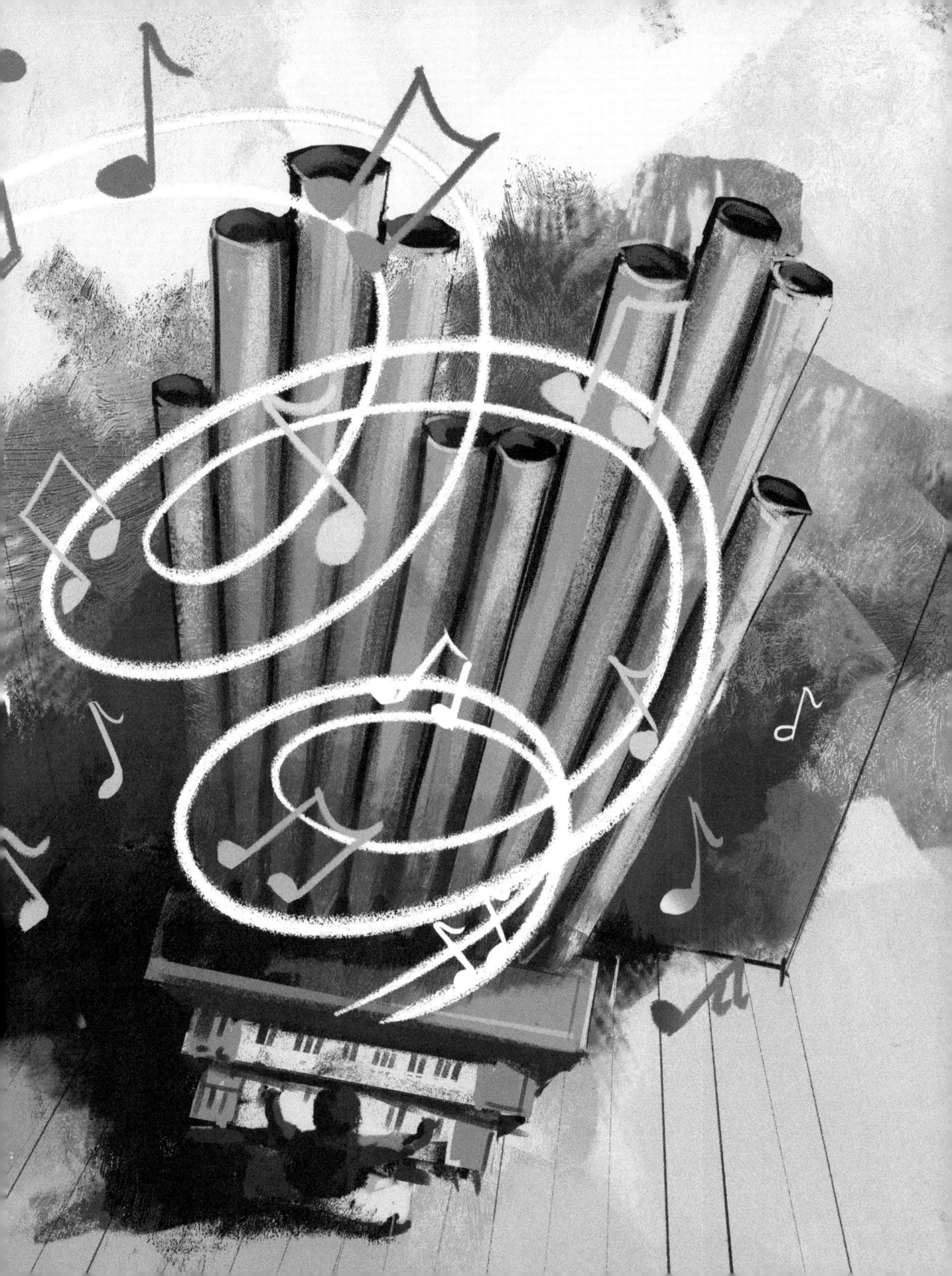

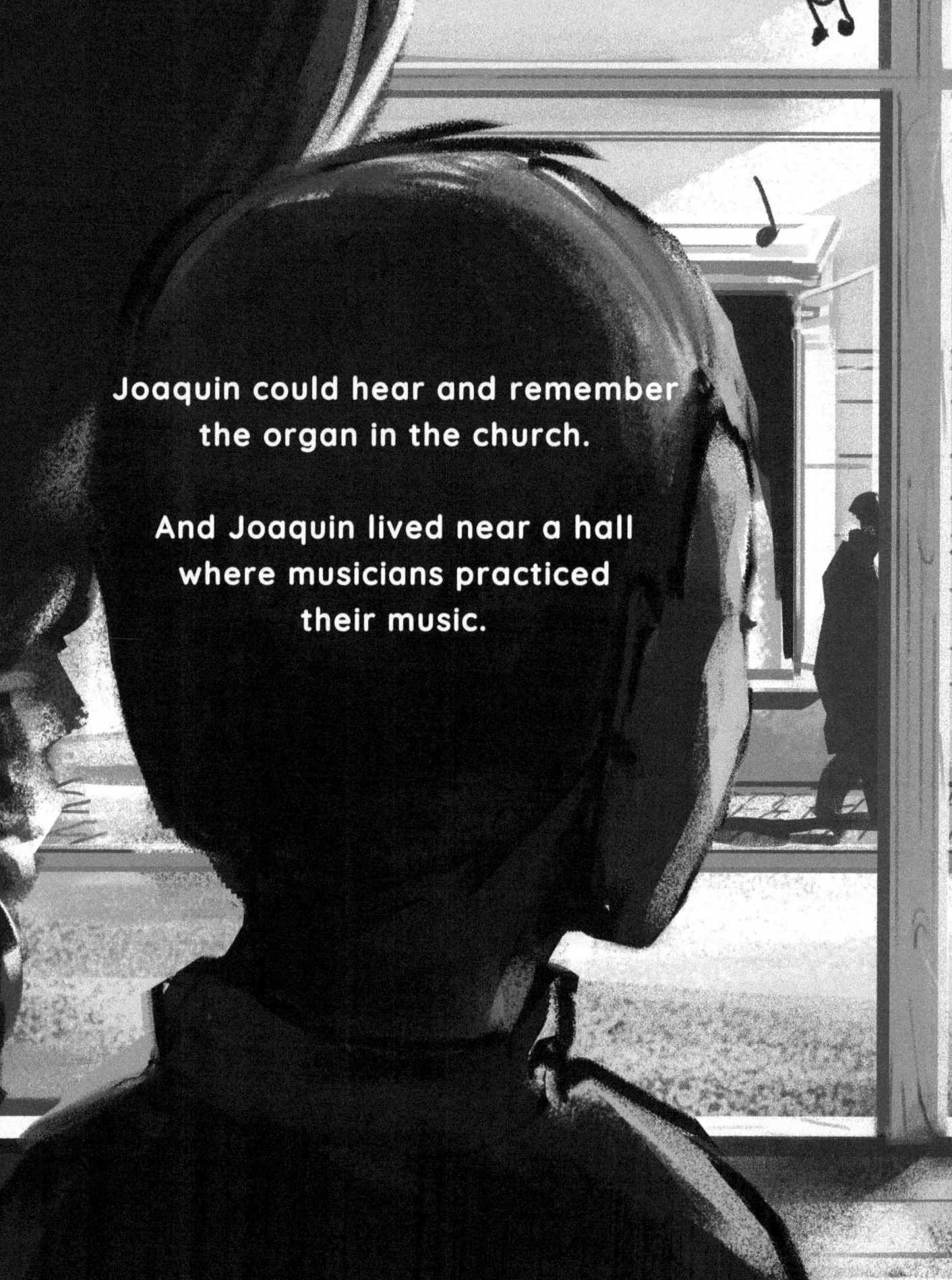

Joaquin could hear and remember
the organ in the church.

And Joaquin lived near a hall
where musicians practiced
their music.

He could hear them playing the piano, and
the violin. He could hear a whole chorus singing.
He spent hours listening to the practicing,
and then to the concerts the musicians gave.

Then, when Joaquin was 4 years old, he and his parents and his brothers and sisters

moved to the big city of Valencia.

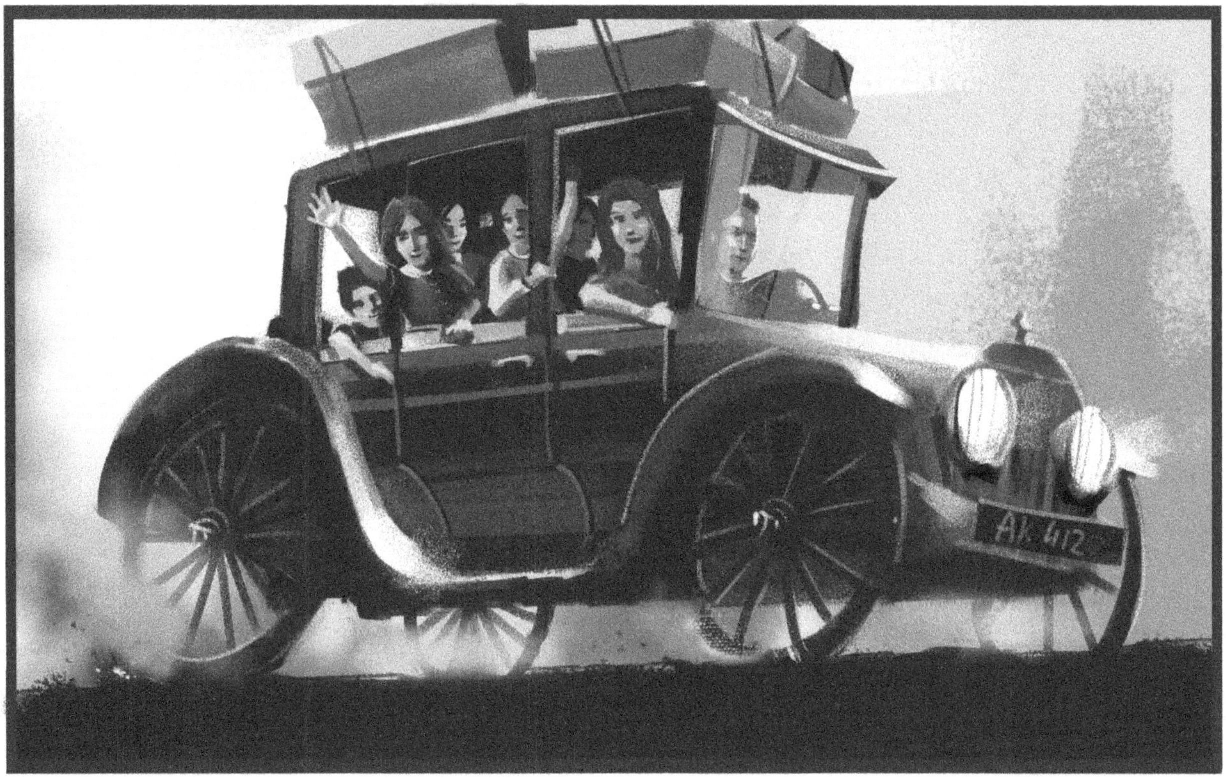
AK 412

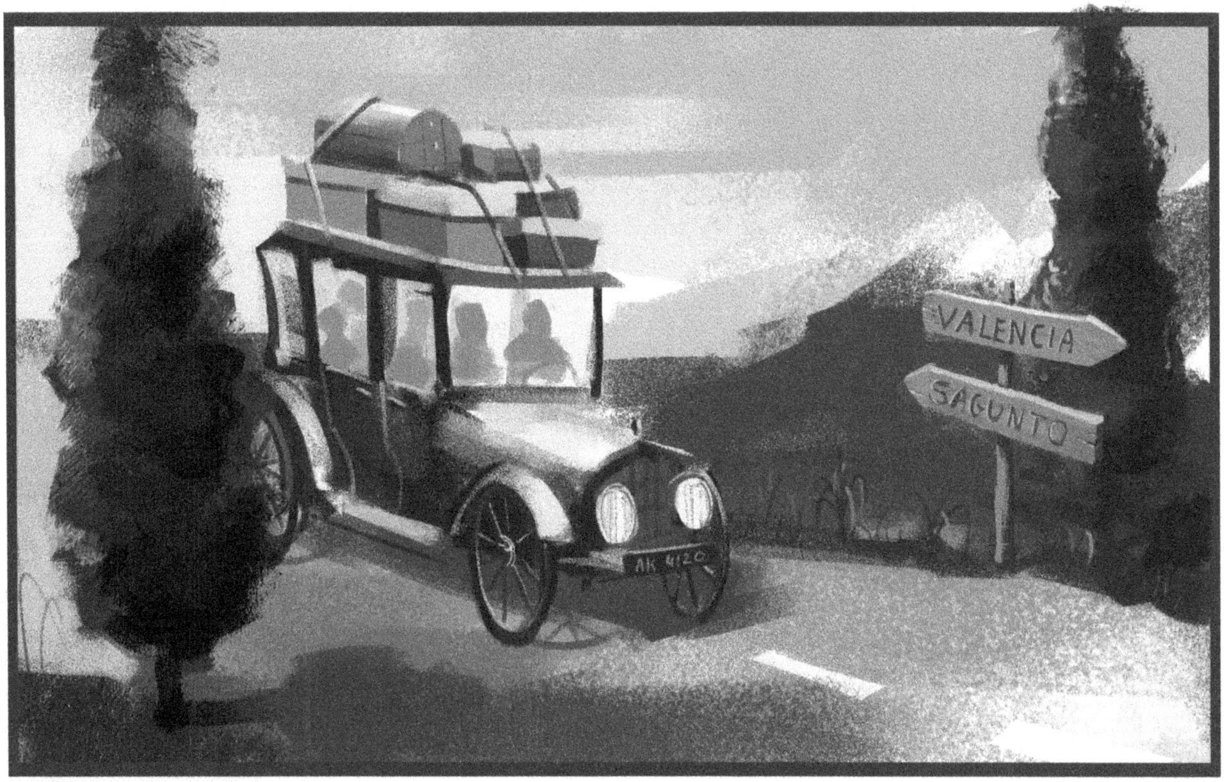
VALENCIA
SAGUNTO

In Valencia, there was a school for blind children. Joaquin started going to school. At school, he got to hear lots of music.

Joaquin and his parents and brothers and sisters started going to the Apollo Theatre. It put on many plays, and musicians played along with the performances.

Joaquin loved to listen to the music!

When Joaquin was 8 years old, he started taking piano lessons. He learned to play the piano and the violin.

Soon he was able to study with teachers from the great Valencia Conservatory. He became a wonderful pianist.

By the time he was 21 years old, Joaquin was writing his own music. Since he couldn't see to write down the notes, he used braille.

Braille is an alphabet made of dots, different patterns for different letters, raised up on paper. Joaquin wrote down music with a special kind of braille that had patterns of dots for musical notes.

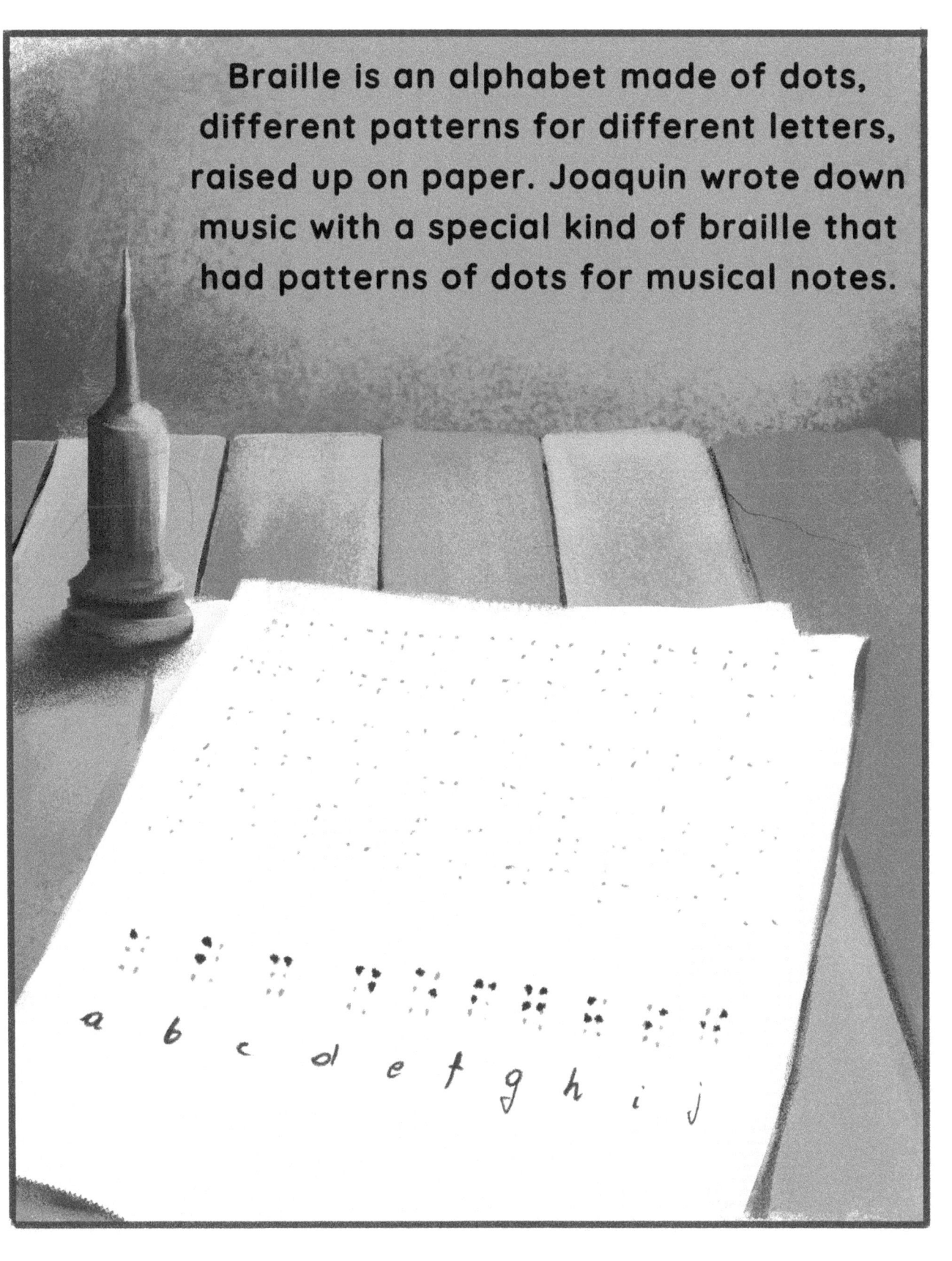

None of his friends
and companions could
read musical braille, so
he dictated the music to
them, note by note.

Then they
wrote it down.

One of his first popular compositions was all about children. The music drew pictures of children running around a playground, getting sleepy after story time, and praying.
He also wrote music meant for children to perform.

Joaquin became a great and famous composer. He wrote pieces for piano, violin, chorus, and guitar.

One of his most famous pieces is
for guitar and orchestra,
even though he didn't
play the guitar.

He even wrote
music for
movies.

Joaquin married a woman who
was also a great pianist.
They had a daughter,
and grandchildren.

Joaquin said that if he hadn't gone blind, he might never have learned to play and write music.

And Joaquin said that in heaven,
we all, every one of us,
will become sounds.

Beautiful sounds.

AWARDS AND HONORS

Joaquin Rodrigo won many awards and honors. These included the Great Cross of Alfonso X el Sabio, the French Légion d'Honneur (Legion of Honor), national music prizes, gold medals, honorary doctorates . . . and many more.

SOURCES OF INSPIRATION

Many of Rodrigo's compositions were inspired by traditional Spanish music. These compositions included, among others, *Muy graciosa es la doncella* (How lovely is the maiden) for voice and piano; the song cycle *Cuatro Madrigales Amatorios* (Four Madrigals of Love); *Concierto Andaluz* for four guitars and orchestra; and his most famous work, *Concierto de Aranjuez* for guitar and orchestra. The *Concierto de Aranjuez* was named after the Royal Palace of Aranjuez and its gardens on the shores of the Tagus River, which flows through Spain and Portugal.

THE VICTORIA AND JOAQUIN RODRIGO FOUNDATION

After Joaquin Rodrigo died, his daughter Cecilia established the Victoria and Joaquin Rodrigo Foundation. Her goal was to make sure Rodrigo's music would be preserved, and would continue to be played and distributed throughout the world. The Foundation uses the Rodrigos' apartment as a museum and a research archive. It also sponsors prizes for the performance of Rodrigo's compositions and for research into his life and music. It received a special prize in 2003 for supporting young musical performers.

MUSICAL BRAILLE

The braille alphabet uses six dots arranged in three rows of two. Musical braille uses letters of that alphabet to stand for notes. The letter "d" stands for the musical note C, the letter "e" stands for the musical note D, and so on up through "j" for the musical note B. The notes are shown in the top two rows, while different symbols for the rhythm of the music appear in the lowest row.

Here's a scale in musical braille.

ACTIVITIES

If you can see, close your eyes and pay attention to everything you can sense. If you can't see, you can close your eyes or not, as you choose.
--What do you hear -- birds, cars, wind, a dog's bark, someone singing or playing music?

--What do you smell -- grass, car exhaust, bread baking, sunshine on grass, someone's perfume?
--What do you feel -- breeze on your skin, a soft or hard chair under you, warm sunshine, chilly air conditioning, the book in your hands?

Listen to music, especially guitar music, Spanish music, or Rodrigo's music. How does it make you feel?

If you can find a guitar, pluck the strings, and strum them, and listen to how they sound. If you press the fingers of your other hand on different parts of the guitar neck, how does that change the sound of the strings?

Try some other musical instrument you've never played before. See what sounds you can make with it.

Make up a tune.

If you can see, look up the braille alphabet or the braille musical alphabet. Use a piece of paper and something with a dull point, like a wooden pencil that isn't too sharp, and press down on the paper to write some braille. You'll be able to read it from the other side (though it'll be backwards). Try reading it with your eyes and with your fingers.

Now try writing it backwards so it'll be the right way around when you read it!

www.ingramcontent.com/pod-product-compliance
Lightning Source LLC
Chambersburg PA
CBHW041154120626
46547CB00020B/3211